Table of Contents

Part I - Credits / Homage
- Dedication............... page a
- Copyright Page .... page b
- Table of Contents .... page c
- Acknowledgments Pt. 2............... page d
- Acknowledgments........................... page e

Part II - Introduction
- Photo of Author and Mother............... [x]
- Kimnicki .... [1]

Part III - Poems
- Anna Mae Bullock..... [2]
- seen it before...................... [3]
- Netflix Movies and Films........ [4]
- Imperfect Wish.... .... [5]
- Mental Health Day .... [6]
- Wi-Fi Not Connected.............................. [7]
- Rated R for hard R................................ [8]
- Yn Class of 2025' .... [9]
- Clorox pt.1. .... [10]

- Clorox pt.2 .... [11]
- not able to send ....[12]
- Masked Truth ....[13]
- Blocked Again ....[14]
- Does it matter? ....[15]
- Panem ....[16]
- ~~Shimie Shimie~~ Shimei ....[17]

Part IV - Vol .2 Coming Soon... [18]

- Still Typing -
  traditional 5 line Kimberly ....[18a]

- First Person or Second -
  a non-traditional 5 line Kimberly... [18b]

- Beauty is- -
  a Kimmy boo style ....[18c]

- the one who spoke to Jeremiah ....[19]
- i write ....[20]
- Missed Call .... [21]
- clorox pt6 I My neighbors Roach ....[22]
- Airplane Mode ....[23]
- Charger Wars ....[24]
- My neighbors Roach pt8 .... [25]

Dedication

This edition is dedicated to my aunt, St. Victoria Williams.

May God bless your soul.

and Let us be grateful for the time we were gifted, and not be sad or saddened by the time we no longer have.

```
"When I was young, my mama used to say,
                 boy
         A woman's like a flower,
       with love on her you shower

              Ever since that day,
            her words never went away
             I always will remember
           to treat my baby tender..—

            ...Treat her like a lady"

                 The Temptations
              "Treat her like a lady"
```

JAY B. WILLIAMS

blah blah blah poem. Vol.1
the manuscript

*First published by
Staten House 2025*

Copyright © 2025 by Jay B. Williams

First edition

*ISBN (paperback): 979-8-90046-054-3
ISBN (hardcover): 979-8-90046-220-2*

Editing: Jay B. Williams
Proofreading: Jay B. Williams
Design & Layout: Jay B. Williams
Content Writing: Jay B. Williams
Illustrations & Cover Art: Jay B. Williams
Style of Poetry (Kimnicki) — Creator: Jay B. Williams
Typesetting: Jay B. Williams

*This book was professionally typeset with assistance by
Reedsy.com*

Copyright © 2025 by Jay B. Williams

All rights reserved. No part of this publication may be reproduced, stored or transmitted in any form or by any means, electronic, mechanical, photocopying, recording, scanning, or otherwise without written permission from the author. It is illegal to copy this book, post it to a website, or distribute it by any other means without permission.

Jay B. Williams asserts the moral right to be identified as the author of this work.

Before July 29, 2025 there was no form known as "Kimnicki." Further, the Form featuring the final phrase *Blah blah blah poem.* Nor has there ever been anyone who has ever claimed ownership of the phrase or any other phrase for the purposes of trade. nor did anyone or entity exist as a trademark featuring the phrase beforementioned prior to this date of claim and or publication date. all phrasing related to the form known as Kimnicki are the original and authentic Protected expressions of pen named author Jay B. Williams born as Jamar Byrd in Southeast, Washington, DC.

Jay B. Williams has no responsibility for the persistence or accuracy of URLs for external or third-party Internet Websites referred to in this publication and does not guarantee that any content on such Websites is, or will remain, accurate or appropriate.

Jay B. Williams asserts that this work is a 1st Amendment protected action, in that it is his right to protest members of the current sitting Congress of the United States of America for its knowing negligence and misappropriation of monies collected through tax, which has and aggregately is becoming more of a detriment to its citizens.

- My neighbors Roach pt 1O .... [26]
- Student: Byrd-Bey .... [27]
- Smoke Alarm Sermon .... [28]
- To See and Not See .... [29]
- man woman and their child .... [30]
- The Algorithm knows .... [31]
- her eyes .... [32]
- Like LL CxxxJay .... [33]
- Rededication .... [34]
- seen by you .... [35]

Final words until next time
Page [36]

Acknowledgments Pt2

There are so many people I want to acknowledge—people who played a role in helping me become the person and artist you see today. I couldn't have done this alone, and I need you to know that their contributions are a part of everything I do.

First and foremost, I thank **My Lord**, who sent **my Lord** to be an example of how I should serve God's people.

I give thanks and honor to all my **ancestors**, **harbingers**, and everyone who came before me—because of you, I was able to be born. I walk in your footsteps, and I carry your legacy forward.

Honors and Respect to the family of Elina Jones—

may she rest in peace.

Da Biggest Shoutout to my Muva Kim.

Ma, I love you. Never forget that. Love, and love more. and before you start nagging me bout how many words dis person or that person got. Remember, the whole thing named after you so calm down. Love you

Obligitory Shoutout to my Pops

I appreciate you ▮▮▮▮▮▮▮▮ and getting my muva ▮▮▮▮▮▮▮▮ Thats gotta be one of the nicest things anybody ever done for me. real talk. I dont know where id be without you. stay blessed.

Shoutout to "The Team [of]Rockets."

I mean Yall aint my kids-kids but i love yall anyway. i hope that counts.

Honorary shoutout to my Grandad Jay

Love you Grandad. I never seen you down for too long. No matter what happens you will find a way. You taught me about a lot of things in your talk and you showed me a lot of things in your walk. Of all the many lessons ive learned watching you the two that hold the most value for me is that: A Man is a Father to his Family, and That it is Manly to Love God.

Thanks Grandad

Honorary Shoutout to my Great Grandad Corneal Byrd

Hey Grandad, Love you. Its Jay, -Kim Son I just wanted to say Thank You for being my Grandad and Giving me my Name. Thank for Being here for me to tell you

Honors & Respect to My GreatGran-Mother Lula Thompson.

I can't believe it's been over 10years since I held your hand. Although we had a very close relationship, these days the memories fade — but I'll never forget that any given Sunday, I could escape whatever was going on in my life and find you on 9th and D.st in Northeast at
The Way of the Cross Baptist Church.

You'd be there with open arms, a welcoming smile, and a warm embrace. In tough times, I run back to those memories— to remind myself what it felt like seeing you come from around the corner and light up when you saw me. I miss those days, all those years ago.

-May God bless your soul.

Honorary Shoutout to my Grandma Betty
Hey Granma i miss you very much. Love you. and get well soon so i can come visit.

Much Love & Respect to Ms Kim
Words will never do justice to the personal and direct impact you had on my life. Not just you, but your entire family. You recognized my innocence and even fought me to protect it. I love you because you didn't have to—but you did. You did more than some who I felt should have — and you did it with patience and grace. You taught me:
"Nothing beats a failure, but a try."
And to
stay away from
F*** N****s". Hahaaa,
Where would I be if I never knew someone like you could believe in me? I guess the world will never know.

Shoutout to the Forever Mayor, Marion S. Barry. Sr

Without the resources, relationships, and leader- ship you brought from Mississippi to Washington, D.C., I'm not sure I'd be standing here today.

Your work laid the foundation for opportunities I've had—not just as a youth, but throughout my life and career as an scholar then a teacher, a community member, writer, artist, and most importantly as a Brother to My people.

-Your impact lives on.

Staff, Students, and Administrators of Birney Elementary (*2000-2007*)

Man, the amount of stuff I put some of these people through is crazy. I just want to give much love to the family of Mrs. Parker. I was a lot to handle as a kid, but she was always patient with me and always loving.

She used to say, "They say you bad — you not bad, you just need a lil' TLC." Then she'd look me in the eyes and ask, "You want some TLC?" And I'd say, "Yes." LOL.

After all these years, I finally found out she was asking me if i wanted her to give me a whoopin'. God bless that lady.

Mr. Steve "Tipper" Burton & David Proctor

What happens in Room 316 stays in Room 316—that's a fact! A lot of us—especially the fellas—we didn't have fathers. We didn't have strong, positive, productive men in our lives who were speaking truth, being real, and guiding us with love and respect. i wanna say that I appreciate you both. Thank you both for showing us what respect looks like. Thank you both for teaching us how to respect ourselves, and how to respect one another.

Growing up in D.C., I was part of a program- called **Mini United Nations**. Me—a kid born in **Greater Southeast Community Hospital** in the '90s—got to walk into an *embassy*, sit across from an *ambassador*, eat with them, and talk with them. That kind of experience was *unheard of* where I'm from. And to this day, people still can't believe it happened.

But   It   Did.

Because of programs like that—and because of
people like Burton and Proctor and Even
Mr. Masantos—we saw the world open up just a
little more than we thought possible. It took
almost 20 years but im here to say,
"Thank You".

Aunt Lorrie
Thanks for pressing me to read that Paul Laurence Dunbar poem all those years ago —   "We Wear the Mask." You know, for a long time I pretended like I understood
why you made me read that poem.
I feel like now is a safe time to tell you — till this day I am L O S T as to what made you share this with me. But I wanted to protect what i felt was a bond we shared through our love for poetry and rap. so i gotta say I appreciate you wanting to give something to your nephew that you felt would help me along my way. because it made me never give up on the idea of being a man who appreciated poetry.
That had to be the first poem request anyone gave me — and because of that, I feel obligated to highlight your contribution to my newfound career as an author and poet.

Life Coach Georggetta Howie
Shoutout to Georggetta Howie-wherever you are in life, stay blessed. Thank you for taking me to Busboys and Poets that time. That moment stuck with me.

The Potters House DC

as a teen i used to go here there was a woman name Mead a unusual name so unusual i dont know if that was even her name... she handed me pottery clay... Thank You

Darick, Thomas, Ms.Queenie, Fred, AnneMarie & The Street Sense Media Organization

i was homeless, Sleeping on the streets, ashamed to talk about it, afraid to embarrass the people that turned they back on me. but after meeting all the wonderful people at street sense media i decided that i dont really care to protect people image i need to tell my story. i was really starving, i was really cold, and really hungry. and the people who could do something to affect change didnt but street sense provided me a outlet and a way to express myself which is priceless. Thanks Thomas and the street sense family.

Michael Kalmbach and the staff at The Creative Vision Factory

I definitely want to thank you all for the impact you've had on my outlook on mental health, and for helping shape my approach to coping and growth. The strategies I've learned for working through challenges have been invaluable, and I'm sure many people in the mental health field will continue to benefit from the proven techniques developed at the Creative Vision Factory.

Commissioner Samuel j Pastore

what can i say man, i rocks wit you because of all those time we worked together to remove barriers to civil engagement such as food, water, clothing, hygiene & feminine hygiene products, as well as civic educational materials.

Andrew Carnegie & DC Public Library System

In 1896, Washington, D.C. began developing its first public library system by establishing reading rooms and book collections in people's homes and community spaces. By 1903, the city's first dedicated library building—funded by Andrew Carnegie—opened to the public, marking a turning point in access to knowledge for the everyday person.

Between 1883 and 1929, Carnegie donated over $56 million to fund the construction of 2,509 libraries across the English-speaking world. Adjusted for inflation, that's more than $1.3 billion invested in learning, literacy, and public empowerment.

For me, those libraries meant something deeply personal. They gave me the confidence to leave school in the 9th grade—not because I didn't value education, but because I understood something most didn't:

The information I needed was already out there. I had access. I just had to choose to seek it. Carnegie once said, "A library outranks any other one thing a community can do to benefit its people." And for someone like me—from where I come from—that access made all the difference.

i foresureski
wanna acknowledge the following people
because it wouldnt be right
if i didnt.
Tyshawn i Love You, shoutout lil black, and my lil baby sister Ivy, My niece lil babyshay, Big shoutout to my Lil Cuzzooooo Spank Dawg & Jaz, My big cuz Dan and Cherry, shoutout Boo, Crystal, and my cuz Ebony.
love all yall
Rip Granma, Rip Shainna, Rip Juju, Rip TC,
Rip Uncle Rick Dawg

S/o My Cousin Aunt Glo & My Cousin's Renee & Danielle, s/o Bonnie, Caren, Brett, my man Ugochukwu Okonkwu(Nick), Big Josh, Mirna, and Samantha. i appreciate yall support and helping me survive 2023-2024

Dre keep your head up love you lil cuzzo

and for ANYBODY the ink didnt mention:
know that youre in my heart and i got you in the next one

With love,
Lil Jay Jay

Acknowledgments
A Special Thank You to My Granny Violetta

Thank you for never giving up on me—no matter what anyone said.
You stood by me through it all, and for that, I'm forever grateful.
Thank you for showing me that it's never too late to try again.
You taught me that people can change, and that real love means making sacrifices that don't always feel good—sacrifices made for family, and for the future.
Thank you for showing me what it means to endure.
Thank you for never giving up on yourself, and for inspiring me to pay attention to the details.
You were my strength and encouragement in the times when I didn't feel strong or motivated.
When I was at my lowest, you were there. I will never forget that.

I love you—always.

Part I
The Introduction

Photo of Author and his Mother

Kimnicki

Kimnicki is a poetic form created by The Author, named in honor of his mother. The traditional form consists of *four lines*, with the *last two lines* always fixed as:

blah blah blah,
Poem.

This framing explicitly identifies the work as a Kimnicki and reflects the form's core idea: a poem that acknowledges its own limitations as merely an idea.
The author describes the Kimnicki as a meditation on meaning, irony, and the boundaries of language itself.

poems in this style are typically humorous or proverbial in some way. However, it mindful to understand that the form of one kimnicki may be a completely different tone of another kimnicki. Some may be dark, some may be scary some may be light hearted others inspirational.

Part II

AnnaMae Bullock

They call it Nutbush! Nutbush, Tennessee.
it's a real place...like...there's people who live there
blah blah blah
poem.

seen it before

im protecting my time
i dont wanna waste it dealing with YOUR things.
blah blah blah
poem.

Nexflix Movies and films

i wonder if Jeffrey Dahmer ever got nervous?
Did anyone ever say "Jeff, just be yourself?"
blah blah blah
poem.

Imperfect Wish

I'm not perfect, I wish I was
Then I'd be able to accept that you are the way you are
blah blah blah
poem.

Mental Health Day

i took a mental health day from work
I spent it working on being okay
blah blah blah
poem.

Wi-Fi not connected

i spent the day with my thoughts, and i realized,
it's ok that sometimes we don't agree
blah blah blah
poem.

Rated R for hard R

like that one name on harry potter
dont say it
blah blah blah
poem.

Yn Class of 2025'

Loose lips sink ships is what I say,
But these days I figure the kids must like swimming.
blah blah blah
poem.

clorox pt 1

clorox is also used as roach spray
atleast it was a few moments ago
blah blah blah
poem.

clorox pt 2

you know raid does a good job
but its so one dimensional
blah blah blah
poem.

not able to send!

too many words
tooo many characters
blah blah blah
poem.

Masked Truth

The night hides the scars that daylight dares to expose.
"Honey, have you seen my mask?"
blah blah blah
poem.

Blocked Again

i thought about texting you again
but then i remembered blocked you last week
blah blah blah
poem.

Does It Matter?

"Does it matter? 'Of course you shall say 'yes,
'But it is of no matter otherwise,' you cruel lover of mine."
blah blah blah
poem.

Panem

beginning in 2020 i learned
alot of my friends were in the audience
blah blah blah
poem.

~~shimie shimie~~ Shimei

B**** A** N*** stole my wallet...
but maybe it was God that sent that man.
blah blah blah
poem.

Part IV

V_{ol.2} Coming Soon

This book, Blah blah blah poem. Vol.1: The Manuscript is a collection of chosen kimnicki that I, the creator and author of this style, felt would best illustrate the core intention and idea vested in its formation.

Those intentions are:
If you do not understand anything about the poem, please still acknowledge that it is a poem and that I am saying something as
the author. I am referencing history I am documenting a moment, a people, a thought, even an event that some may have had no other reason to learn about. Irregardless I am speaking to be understood, expecting that you are listening to understand.

     Sincerly
Jay B. williams

But even then, no matter how much I explain,
my words won't be understood
blah blah blah
poem.

...Still Typing
(a traditional 5-line Kimberly)

```
you were typing for five minutes
30      deleted     sentences      later
typing...
blah blah blah
poem.
```

First Person or Second?
(a Non Traditional 5-Line Kimberly)

```
    why do you love me?
the image in the glass said to me
    why do you love me?
       blah blah blah

          poem.
```

Beauty is-
(Kimmy Boo style)

```
Your Smile is beautiful

your smile beautiful

not just because it's on your
beautiful face

to me
your smile is beautiful
your smile is beautiful to me
not just because it shines and glows

but because of how-
how?
-how it makes me feel
blah blah blah
poem.
```

the one who spoke to Jeremiah

"plagiarism is THEFT." they say
yet they still wont acknowledge you.
blah blah blah
poem.

i write

sometimes i write;
sometimes its because i dont want to forget i loved you
blah blah blah
poem.

Missed Call

i didn't answer your call on purpose
I got upset when you didn't call again
blah blah blah
poem.

clorox pt6 / my neighbor's roach

i live in fear of my neighbor's roaches.
that's a weird phrase.
blah blah blah
poem.

Airplane Mode

i pretended to be in the sky
I had to avoid your gravity
blah blah blah
poem.

Charger Wars

I gave her my last percent now im dead,
and still alone.
blah blah blah
poem.

my neighbors roach pt 8

the leasing office said
they need proof of trespassing.
blah blah blah
poem.

my neighbors roach pt 10

wow, so now we goin pretend
i dont have a right to defend my home.
blah blah blah
poem.

Student: Byrd-Bey

there is, is' and there is, aint'.
Know the difference.
blah blah blah
poem.

Smoke Alarm Sermon

i once lit incense to pray
but then the smoke alarm started preaching
blah blah blah
poem.

To See and Not See

To see and not see, to hear and not hear,
Is to perceive, and yet to not be perceived as perceiving.
blah blah blah
poem.

man woman and child

eight-thousand; five-hundred; two and thirty pennies.
this revolution will not be televized
blah blah blah
poem.

The Algorithm Knows

i said i was over you
then youtube suggested "so sick" by NE-yo
blah blah blah
poem.

her eyes

damn i could stare all day
im not doe, cuz its weird
blah blah blah
poem.

like LL Cxxx J

If i lick my lips like this...
can i ask you out?
blah blah blah
poem.

seen by you

i love the way
it feels to be seen by you
blah blah blah
poem.

Rededication

Words unsaid, yet deeply and intimately known,
We rededicate ourselves to one another.
blah blah blah
poem.

Final Words from our Author

- Why is there Kimnicki? -

Kimnicki exists because every generation gotta have something of its own time.

Tha world in which I have seen; it needs structure born of truth. Uncut unadulterated and yet still refined.

Kimnicki is that structure.

At its core, Kimnicki symbolizes the act of:

speaking to be understood.

It carries the tension between hope and reality -
tha hope that listeners will understand, and the reality that many will dismiss it as

"blah blah blah,
[another] poem."

Kimnicki is built on discipline.
Every line matters. Nothing is wasted.
It is not clutter, not noise, not filler.

It is brevity sharpened into impact.

For More Info about the author

V.1

please scan

or visit
Linktr.ee/JayBwilliams

The author Jay B. Williams sells his first work as a author titled -"Be Brave (and thanks to those who have been.)" a piece written in memory of his father who served in the armed forces.

The author outside of The Auditorium at Dr. Martin Luther King Jr Memorial Library in Washington, D.C. Attending the premiere of "Free The People" a film by Kintsugi Kelley-Chung & Andrew Jasiura collectively know as "Rxnin Life"

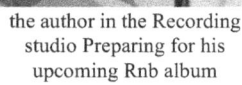

the author in the Recording studio Preparing for his upcoming Rnb album

"Unrequitted Love Songs 4 Tha Streets"

Understanding

Where's Relisha Rudd

the

Where's
Relisha Rudd

hill

Where's Relisha Rudd

you're

Where's Relisha Rudd

standing

Where's
Relisha
Rudd

on

Where's
Relisha
Rudd

begins

*Where's
Relisha
Rudd*

with

Where's Relisha Rudd

a

Where's Relisha Rudd

clear

Where's Relisha Rudd

look

Where's Relisha Rudd

at

Where's Relisha Rudd

cause

Where's Relisha Rudd

you

Where's
Relisha
Rudd

choose

Where's Relisha Rudd

to

Where's Relisha Rudd

defend.

Where's
Relisha Rudd

In

Where's Relisha Rudd

moments

**Where's
Relisha
Rudd**

of

**Where's
Relisha Rudd**

decision,

*<u>Where's
Relisha Rudd</u>*

take

Where's Relisha Rudd

time

Where's
Relisha
Rudd

to

Where's
Relisha
Rudd

measure

Where's Relisha Rudd

whether

Where's Relisha Rudd

that hill is

*Where's
Relisha Rudd*

-or that hill is not

Where's Relisha Rudd

worthy

_____
____

Where's Relisha Rudd

of

Where's Relisha Rudd

your effort

or

your

sacrifice.

Where's Relisha Rudd

Not

**Where's
Relisha Rudd**

every

Where's Relisha Rudd

dispute

Where's Relisha Rudd

demands

Where's Relisha Rudd

everythang

Where's Relisha Rudd

that

**Where's
Relisha Rudd**

you

Where's Relisha Rudd

have -,

Where's Relisha Rudd

-but some principles and personal convictions to said principles at some point will compel you to do so.

Where's Relisha Rudd

-and

Where's Relisha Rudd

when

*Where's
Relisha
Rudd*

they do

Where's Relisha Rudd

bring to mind
this
Latin maxim

Where's Relisha Rudd

Fiat iustitia, ruat caelum

Where's Relisha Rudd

remember

the phrase is

Fiat iustitia, ruat caelum

———

Where's Relisha Rudd

Let

Where's Relisha Rudd

justice

Where's Relisha Rudd

be

Where's
Relisha
Rudd

done.....

Let justice be done...

Where's Relisha Rudd

though

Where's Relisha Rudd

the heavens fall.

Where's
Relisha Rudd

Choose

Where's Relisha Rudd

your hill...

Where's Relisha Rudd

Choose your hill......

with purpose,

Where's Relisha Rudd

Choose your hill......

    with purpose,

                with conviction,

<u>Where's Relisha Rudd</u>

Choose your hill......

    with purpose,

                    with conviction,

and with an unwavering commitment....-

Where's Relisha Rudd

Choose your hill with purpose, conviction, and an unwavering commitment to what truly matters.

Where's Relisha Rudd

In moments of decision, it's crucial to evaluate the causes we choose to defend. Not every dispute requires all our energy, but certain principles and personal convictions may, at times, demand our full commitment. When that happens, remember the Latin maxim:

Fiat iustitia, ruat caelum — "Let justice be done, though the heavens fall." Choose your hill wisely, with purpose and unwavering conviction. Stand firm for what truly matters, and be prepared to sacrifice for those principles that shape who you are and what you believe in.

November 20, 2025

www.ingramcontent.com/pod-product-compliance
Lightning Source LLC
Chambersburg PA
CBHW031347160426
43196CB00007B/756